ENCYCLICAL LETTER
PACEM IN TERRIS
OF HIS HOLINESS
POPE JOHN XXIII

*

Message for the Celebration
of the World Day of Peace 2003
of His Holiness
POPE JOHN PAUL II

LIBRERIA EDITRICE VATICANA
00120 VATICAN CITY

Pacem in terris:

Original Latin text in *Acta Apostolicae Sedis* (AAS) 55 (1963) 257-304.
English text: *Pacem in Terris,* Catholic Truth Society, London 2002.
English translation: *The Pope Speaks,* 9 (1963) 13-48.

PREFACE

"In Christianity time has a fundamental importance" (*Tertio millennio adveniente*, 10).

For the Holy See, therefore, the presentation of a new edition of the Encyclical *Pacem in terris*, which Blessed Pope John XXIII published 40 years ago, is not a simple formality.

With this editorial release, the pontifical document is proposed, once again, for the reading and reflection of all people of good will.

Unfortunately, what the beginning of this millennium and the climate of the 1960s have in common is a widespread sense of fear. "[P]eople are living in the grip of constant fear", wrote Pope John XXIII. "They are afraid that at any moment the impending storm may break upon them with horrific violence" (*Pacem in terris*, 111). This was the atmosphere in a world preyed upon by the arms race and the nuclear threat. With no less effective words, Pope John Paul II describes the sense of personal insecurity that pervaded everyone when, on 11 September 2001, the phenomenon of terrorism exploded in all its horror: "Since then, people throughout the world have felt a profound personal vulnerability and a new fear for the future" (*2002 World Day of Peace Message*, n. 1).

It is as if ideologies, which fell symbolically with the collapse of the Berlin Wall, came to construct another wall of incomprehension to divide the world still further, contributing to a permanent situation of disorder and fear which all are able to observe.

To the fundamental question of what kind of order can replace this disorder in the era of globalization, in which the world is nevertheless "organizing" itself, another question is added and that is on what principles are these new forms of world order developing (cf.. John Paul II, *2003 World Day of Peace Message*, n. 6).

Rereading *Pacem in terris* helps to recall the unavoidable requirements for the construction of such an order, which cannot ignore ethics and must be founded on the four pillars of truth, justice, charity and freedom. Such requirements are born from respect for human dignity and human rights, from observance of the respective duties, from awareness of belonging to the world community formed from one human family. This is why it is desirable to have a global authority not imposed by force, but instituted by common agreement among national authorities that maintain relations with it according to the principle of subsidiarity (cf.. *Pacem in terris*, 138 and 140).

It is also true that such a process can only take place in the context of hope that, in the spirituality of Blessed John XXIII, assumed the aspect of Christian optimism and, in the formation of the current Holy Father John Paul II, assumes the courage of the disciples of He who said: "Be brave: I have conquered the world" (*John* 16:33).

The Vatican, 24 June, Feast of the Birth of St. John the Baptist.

✠ ANGELO Card. SODANO
Secretary of State

PRESENTATION

During his brief pontificate (1958-1963), Blessed Pope John XXIII was tireless in his pursuit of peace. Peace was among the issues put before the Council, which met 17 years after the end of the Second World War. The Pope invited Bishops representing all peoples and nations, to contribute to "healing and curing the scars of the two conflicts that have profoundly altered the face of all nations. The mothers and fathers of families detest war. The Church, the mother of all without distinction, once more raises the cry which comes from the earliest centuries, from Bethlehem and Calvary, and which now finds expression in a profound plea for a precept of peace that would prevent armed conflicts; a peace that must have its roots and its guarantee in the heart of every person".[1] The Pope's most significant contribution to peace is certainly the encyclical *Pacem in terris*. Published on 11 April 1963, three weeks before his death, the encyclical can be considered the culminating synthesis of a reflection on peace and on the need for a culture of peace that had been developed by the papacy during the turbulent and bloody history of the 20th Century.

A new perspective concerning peace

Pope John XXIII centers his consideration of peace on the principle of the dignity of the human

---

[1] Pope JOHN XXIII, *Radio broadcast to the Christian faithful* (11 September 1962), one month before the Opening of the Second Vatican Council. Official text in: *Concilio Vaticano II. Constitutiones, Decreta, Declarationes*. Libreria Editrice Vaticana, Città del Vaticano 1998, pp. 1084 -1085. The English translation here given is an unofficial translation.

person, which constitutes its indispensable foundation. An order exists which has man at its summit, with his dignity, his rights and his duties. To subvert this order, to fail to recognize the rights and duties of man, means to destroy peace. The Pope wrote in *Pacem in terris*: "Any well-regulated and productive association of men in society demands the acceptance of one fundamental principle: that each individual man is truly a person. His is a nature endowed with intelligence and free will. As such he has rights and duties, which together flow as a direct consequence from his nature. These rights and duties are universal and inviolable, and therefore altogether inalienable".[2]

After having stated that the foundational element of coexistence lies in the dignity of the human person, Blessed John XXIII indicates the essential conditions for peace. These correspond to four precise needs of the human spirit: *truth, justice, love, and freedom.* Pope John Paul II dwells on these conditions, indicating precisely the basic forms of their concrete actualization: "*Truth* will build peace if every individual sincerely acknowledges not only his rights, but also his own duties towards others. *Justice* will build peace if in practice everyone respects the rights of others and actually fulfills his duties towards them. *Love* will build peace if people feel the needs of others as their own and share what they have with others, especially the values of mind and spirit which they possess. *Freedom* will build peace and make it thrive if, in the choice of the means to that end, people act according to reason and assume responsibility for their own actions".[3]

[2] Pope JOHN XXIII, Encyclical Letter *Pacem in terris,* n. 9.
[3] Pope JOHN PAUL II, *Message for the World Day of Peace 2003,* n. 3.

The ideal of peace is treated in the encyclical *Pacem in terris* in the fullness of its positive meaning found in a biblical and theological approach. This does not mean, however, that Blessed John XXIII's reflection does not take into account the problem of institutional mediation as well as political and juridical changes which are necessary if this ideal is to find an effective realization in history. The encyclical, in fact, presents both rational and political arguments concerning the need for peace, together with analyses and reflections on the waste of resources in the arms race. It also addresses social justice in a worldwide perspective, the interdependence of peoples, the exploitive relationship between the North and South, the need to strengthen the United Nations, and the right of peoples to independence. The encyclical also encourages wide-ranging political responsibility, supported by the awareness that peace is not an impossible dream, but an objective possibility inscribed in the historical process.

Pacem in terris gives a warning, which is also dramatically timely for the current international scene, regarding the priority to be given to complete disarmament, not only at the policy level as pertains to armaments, but above all at the cultural level. It is a question of *dismantling* men's very souls, without which "it is impossible to stop the arms race, or to reduce armaments, or – and this is the main thing – ultimately to abolish them entirely. Everyone must sincerely co-operate in the effort to banish fear and the anxious expectation of war from men's minds. But this requires that the fundamental principles upon which peace is based in today's world be replaced by an altogether different one, namely, the realization that true and lasting peace among nations cannot consist in the possession of an equal supply of armaments but only in mutual trust. And We are confident that this can be achieved, for it is a thing which not only is dictated by common sense, but is in itself most desirable and most fruitful of good".[4]

Faced with the risk of a nuclear war, of absolute destruction, the encyclical maintains that in our age, which is hailed as the atomic era, still to consider war a suitable means for restoring violated rights is not rational.[5] The encyclical points out that there is a strong and innovative rupture with regard to preceding reflections, due to a lucid and all-embracing awareness of the new factor represented by the "nuclear revolution". John XXIII is aware of the fact that the balance of terror cannot correspond to "the Church's fifteen-hundred-year-old teaching on peace as *tranquillitas ordinis* – the tranquillity of order' as Saint Augustine called it"[6] and takes a position in favor of complete disarmament. It is precisely the qualitatively new character of nuclear war, with its prospects of global extermination, of the self-destruction of the human race, which makes recourse to war unacceptable and also the very possibility of its continued consideration in terms of *extrema ratio*.

Peace today

The Holy Father, Pope John Paul II, in his *Message for the World Day of Peace 2003,* draws upon the fundamental themes of the teaching of *Pacem in terris* and, at the same time, considers them in the context of the *res novae* of our era. The words of Blessed John XXIII's encyclical on peace are once more proposed forty years later with, in fact, extraordinary timeliness

---

[4] Pope JOHN XXIII, Encyclical Letter *Pacem in terris*, n. 113.
[5] Pope JOHN XXIII, ENCYCLICAL LETTER *Pacem in terris*, nn. 109-119.
[6] Pope JOHN PAUL II, *Message for the World Day of Peace 2003*, n. 6.

and the unchanged power of truth. Their contemporary nature is due both to the *res novae* which today confront the builders of peace and incite all to express, in new ways, the power of peace, as well as to the breadth and depth of the Christian message of peace. Due to its wonderful richness, this message speaks to the hearts of people of every age, even our own, especially when the road to peace is threatened by challenges, and impeded by delays and obstacles that give rise to concern.

If a certain political fundamentalism prevailed forty years ago, today we risk nourishing forms of religious fundamentalism. At the time of *Pacem in terris,* certain ideological visions dramatically conditioned culture and political practice with the establishment of regimes that did not respect the dignity of the human person. In our day, religions manipulated for political purposes are used for ends that profoundly distort their intrinsic truth. In the face of this terrible new threat, all religions must unite in the pursuit of the good of the human person. The true face of religion is disfigured if it becomes an instrument of conflict which people use against one another. The tremendous devastation caused by the horrible terrorist acts of 11 September 2001, and their dramatic aftermath of death and suffering, remain a warning for all.[7]

If rigid opposing blocs endangered peace among nations forty years ago, today a lack of dialogue between States and peoples can do the same. At the time of Blessed John XXIII, dialogue could have been considered an inadequate instrument for overcoming the rigid division of the world into areas of influence. In our times, however, dialogue directed towards bilateral and mul-

---

[7] Cf. Pope JOHN PAUL II, *Message for the World Day of Peace 2002,* n. 6.

tilateral agreements, and the capacity for mediation seen in the highest and most noble sense – that is, as aiming at meeting not only in a spirit of negotiation, but also of reciprocal respect and enrichment – are all the more necessary as the world becomes polycentric and interdependent, even politically. The lack of dialogue and trust in international relations, the lack of respect for commitments and the failure to honor promises are among the principal reasons for the weakening of the cause of peace today.[8]

If, forty years ago, the cause of peace could above all be served by bringing out those differences that had been stifled under the concealing mantle of ideologies and authoritarian and totalitarian regimes, the time has come today to value instead what joins and unites us, as the foundation and measure of these same differences. In certain historical moments, in fact, political relations are better served by the appropriate consideration of how much we are all profoundly similar beyond our differences, and how valuing the differences makes clear the inexhaustible richness of our shared human nature. At times, many individuals and even entire peoples fear this demanding truth. They can conquer this fear by opening their minds to the value of the diversity of others, and by being open to dialogue, but still more by recognizing that all men belong to one family. In doing so, they open themselves to a spirit of service to the human person and his or her universal rights. There is a time for learning from differences; there is a time for learning from what unites us. Today, it is the latter that must take priority.[9]

[8] Cf. Pope JOHN PAUL II, *Message for the World Day of Peace 2003*, n. 8.
[9] Cf. Pope JOHN PAUL II, *Message for the World Day of Peace 2003*, n. 5.

The Gospel of Peace, which John XXIII's encyclical *Pacem in terris* heralded forty years ago and which Pope John Paul II re-proposed in his *Message for the World Day of Peace 2003*, lights the way for men and women even in the face of new challenges to peace that characterize our time. As Pope John Paul II recalled in his Address to the Diplomatic Corps accredited to the Holy See in January 1987, "peace is first of all a gift of God".[10] It is a gift and a promise of Jesus Christ. In fact, Christian peace is Jesus Christ himself, the Son of God made man in order to bring us *his* peace (cf. *Jn* 14, 27), or better still it is the very encounter with him. It is also a promise, since complete peace will be given to us at the end of time. But it is never an abstract peace, projected only in a future far distant from everyday life. It is an historical peace. It originates from a Gift and a Promise that traverse the boundaries of time, but it became an element of daily life and a call to a commitment by all, here and now, given that the Word of God became flesh in Jesus of Nazareth. In the same Address to the Diplomatic Corps mentioned above, the Holy Father teaches that peace "is the fruit of free wills guided by reason towards the common good... In this sense, it seems within the reach of the well-educated and mature man".[11]

Pacem in terris presents peace both as a gift of God and as the fruit of human commitment. Precisely at the convergence of these two dimensions Blessed John XXIII notes the possibility for people to live with neither alienation nor despair the burning issue of peace. In such a perspective, I am happy to present this publication which brings together two fundamen-

---

[10] PONTIFICAL COUNCIL FOR JUSTICE AND PEACE, *John Paul II and the Family of Peoples*, Vatican City 2002, p. 141.

[11] *Ibidem*, p. 141.

tal texts concerning peace: *Pacem in terris* of Blessed John XXIII and *The 2003 Message for the World Day of Peace* of Pope John Paul II which is directly connected to John XXIII's encyclical in both title and content. From these two outstanding texts of the pontifical Magisterium comes the invitation to live the Gospel of Peace. This Gospel awaits a generous response and innumerable *gestures of peace*,[12] which Pope John Paul II continues to advance, both in word and deed.

H.E. Archbishop RENATO RAFFAELE MARTINO
President of the Pontifical Council for Justice and Peace

11 April 2003
40th Anniversary of *Pacem in Terris*

---

[12] Pope JOHN PAUL II, *Message for the World Day of Peace 2003*, n. 9.

ENCYCLICAL LETTER
PACEM IN TERRIS
OF HIS HOLINESS
POPE JOHN XXIII

*On establishing universal peace
in truth, justice, charity and liberty*

To our Venerable Brethren the Patriarchs, Primates,
Archbishops, Bishops, and all other local ordinaries
who are at peace and in communion with the Apostolic See,
and to the Clergy and Faithful of the entire Catholic World,
and to all men of good will

INTRODUCTION

Venerable Brethren and Dearest Sons,
Health and Apostolic Benediction.

1.   Peace on Earth — which man throughout the ages has so longed for and sought after — can never be established, never guaranteed, except by the diligent observance of the divinely established order.

Order in the Universe

2.   That a marvellous order predominates in the world of living beings and in the forces of nature, is the plain lesson which the progress of modern research and the discoveries of technology teach us. And it is part of the greatness of man that he can appreciate that order, and devise the means for harnessing those forces for his own benefit.

3.   But what emerges first and foremost from the progress of scientific knowledge and the inventions of technology is the infinite greatness of God Himself, who created both man and the universe. Yes; out of nothing He made all things, and filled them with the fullness of His own wisdom and goodness. Hence, these are the words the holy psalmist used in praise of God: "O Lord, our Lord: how admirable

is thy name in the whole earth!" [1] And elsewhere he says: "How great are thy works, O Lord! Thou hast made all things in wisdom".[2]

Moreover,[2a] God created man "in His own image and likeness",[3] endowed him with intelligence and freedom, and made him lord of creation. All this the psalmist proclaims when he says: "Thou hast made him a little less than the angels: thou hast crowned him with glory and honour, and hast set him over the works of thy hands. Thou hast subjected all things under his feet".[4]

Order in Human Beings

4. And yet there is a disunity among individuals and among nations which is in striking contrast to this perfect order in the universe. One would think that the relationships that bind men together could only be governed by force.

5. But the world's Creator has stamped man's inmost being with an order revealed to man by his conscience; and his conscience insists on his preserving it. Men "show the work of the law written in their hearts. Their conscience bears witness to them".[5] And how could it be otherwise? All created being reflects the infinite wisdom of God. It reflects it all the more clearly, the higher it stands in the scale of perfection.[6]

---

[1] *Ps* 8:1.

[2] *Ps* 103:24.

[2a] In the Latin text this paragraph is part of the preceding one, hence we have not assigned it a number. For format reasons we have broken paragraphs down in a few places but have kept our numbering system keyed to the Latin paragraphs. Ed. of TPS

[3] Cf. *Gen* 1:26.

[4] *Ps* 8:5-6.

[5] *Rom* 2:15.

[6] Cf. *Ps* 18:8-11.

6.   But the mischief is often caused by erroneous opinions. Many people think that the laws which govern man's relations with the State are the same as those which regulate the blind, elemental forces of the universe. But it is not so; the laws which govern men are quite different. The Father of the universe has inscribed them in man's nature, and that is where we must look for them; there and nowhere else.

7.   These laws clearly indicate how a man must behave toward his fellows in society, and how the mutual relationships between the members of a State and its officials are to be conducted. They show too what principles must govern the relations between States; and finally, what should be the relations between individuals or States on the one hand, and the world-wide community of nations on the other. Men's common interests make it imperative that at long last a world-wide community of nations be established.

I. ORDER BETWEEN MEN

8. We must devote our attention first of all to that order which should prevail among men.

9. Any well-regulated and productive association of men in society demands the acceptance of one fundamental principle: that each individual man is truly a person. His is a nature endowed with intelligence and free will. As such he has rights and duties, which together flow as a direct consequence from his nature. These rights and duties are universal and inviolable, and therefore altogether inalienable.[7]

10. When, furthermore, we consider man's personal dignity from the standpoint of divine revelation, inevitably our estimate of it is incomparably increased. Men have been ransomed by the blood of Jesus Christ. Grace has made them sons and friends of God, and heirs to eternal glory.

Rights

11. But first We must speak of man's rights. Man has the right to live. He has the right to bodily integrity and to the means necessary for the proper development of life, particularly food, clothing, shelter, medical care, rest, and, finally, the necessary social services. In consequence, he has the right to be looked after in the event of ill health; disability stemming from his work; widowhood; old age; enforced

---

[7] Cf. Pius XII, Broadcast message, Christmas 1942, AAS 35 (1943) 9-24; and John XXIII, Sermon, Jan. 4, 1963, AAS 55 (1963) 89-91.

unemployment; or whenever through no fault of his own he is deprived of the means of livelihood.[8]

Rights Pertaining to Moral and Cultural Values

12. Moreover, man has a natural right to be respected. He has a right to his good name. He has a right to freedom in investigating the truth, and — within the limits of the moral order and the common good — to freedom of speech and publication, and to freedom to pursue whatever profession he may choose. He has the right, also, to be accurately informed about public events.

13. He has the natural right to share in the benefits of culture, and hence to receive a good general education, and a technical or professional training consistent with the degree of educational development in his own country. Furthermore, a system must be devised for affording gifted members of society the opportunity of engaging in more advanced studies, with a view to their occupying, as far as possible, positions of responsibility in society in keeping with their natural talent and acquired skill.[9]

The Right to Worship God According to One's Conscience

14. Also among man's rights is that of being able to worship God in accordance with the right dictates of his own conscience, and to profess his religion both in private and in public. According to the clear teaching of Lactantius, "this is the very condition of our birth, that we render to the God who made us that just homage which is His due; that we acknowledge

---

[8] Cf. Pius XI, Encyclical letter *Divini Redemptoris*, AAS 29 (1931) 78; and Pius XII, Broadcast message, Pentecost, June 1, 1941, AAS 33 (1941) 195-205.

[9] Cf. Pius XII, Broadcast message, Christmas 1942, AAS 35 (1943) 9-24.

Him alone as God, and follow Him. It is from this ligature of piety, which binds us and joins us to God, that religion derives its name". [10]

Hence, too, Pope Leo XIII declared that "true freedom, freedom worthy of the sons of God, is that freedom which most truly safeguards the dignity of the human person. It is stronger than any violence or injustice. Such is the freedom which has always been desired by the Church, and which she holds most dear. It is the sort of freedom which the Apostles resolutely claimed for themselves. The apologists defended it in their writings; thousands of martyrs consecrated it with their blood". [11]

The Right to Choose Freely One's State in Life

15. Human beings have also the right to choose for themselves the kind of life which appeals to them: whether it is to found a family — in the founding of which both the man and the woman enjoy equal rights and duties — or to embrace the priesthood or the religious life. [12]

16. The family, founded upon marriage freely contracted, one and indissoluble, must be regarded as the natural, primary cell of human society. The interests of the family, therefore, must be taken very specially into consideration in social and economic affairs, as well as in the spheres of faith and morals. For all of these have to do with strengthening the family and assisting it in the fulfillment of its mission.

---

[10] *Divinae institutiones*, lib. IV, c. 28.2; PL 6.535.

[11] Encyclical letter *Libertas praestantissimum,* Acta Leonis XIII, VIII, 1888, pp. 237-238.

[12] Cf. Pius XII, *Broadcast message, Christmas 1942,* AAS 35 (1943) 9-24.

17. Of course, the support and education of children is a right which belongs primarily to the parents.[13]

Economic Rights

18. In the economic sphere, it is evident that a man has the inherent right not only to be given the opportunity to work, but also to be allowed the exercise of personal initiative in the work he does.[14]

19. The conditions in which a man works form a necessary corollary to these rights. They must not be such as to weaken his physical or moral fibre, or militate against the proper development of adolescents to manhood. Women must be accorded such conditions of work as are consistent with their needs and responsibilities as wives and mothers.[15]

20. A further consequence of man's personal dignity is his right to engage in economic activities suited to his degree of responsibility.[16] The worker is likewise entitled to a wage that is determined in accordance with the precepts of justice. This needs stressing. The amount a worker receives must be sufficient, in proportion to available funds, to allow him and his family a standard of living consistent with human dignity. Pope Pius XII expressed it in these terms: "Nature imposes work upon man as a duty, and man has the corresponding natural right to demand that the work he does shall provide him with the means of livelihood for himself and his children.

[13] Cf. Pius XI, Encyclical letter *Casti connubii*, AAS 22 (1930) 539-592; and Pius XII, Broadcast message, Christmas 1942, AAS 35 (1943) 9-24.

[14] Cf. Pius XII, Broadcast message, Pentecost, June 1, 1941, AAS 33 (1941) 201.

[15] Cf. Leo XIII, *Encyclical letter Rerum novarum*, Acta Leonis XIII, XI, 1891, pp. 128-129.

[16] Cf. John XXIII, Encyclical letter *Mater et Magistra*, AAS 53 (1961) 422.

Such is nature's categorical imperative for the preservation of man".[17]

21.   As a further consequence of man's nature, he has the right to the private ownership of property, including that of productive goods. This, as We have said elsewhere, is "a right which constitutes so efficacious a means of asserting one's personality and exercising responsibility in every field, and an element of solidity and security for family life, and of greater peace and prosperity in the State".[18]

22.   Finally, it is opportune to point out that the right to own private property entails a social obligation as well.[19]

The Right of Meeting and Association

23.   Men are by nature social, and consequently they have the right to meet together and to form associations with their fellows. They have the right to confer on such associations the type of organisation which they consider best calculated to achieve their objectives. They have also the right to exercise their own initiative and act on their own responsibility within these associations for the attainment of the desired results.[20]

24.   As We insisted in Our encyclical *Mater et Magistra*, the founding of a great many such intermediate groups or societies for the pursuit of aims which it is not within the competence of the individual to

[17] Cf. Pius XII, Broadcast message, Pentecost, June 1, 1941, AAS 33 (1941) 201.

[18] John XXIII, Encyclical letter *Mater et Magistra*, AAS 53 (1961) 428.

[19] Cf. *ibid.*, p. 430; TPS v. 7, no. 4, p. 318.

[20] Cf. Leo XIII, Encyclical letter *Rerum novarum*, Acta Leonis XIII, XI, 1891, pp. 134-142; Pius XI, Encyclical letter *Quadragesimo anno*, AAS 23 (1931) 199-200; and Pius XII, Encyclical letter *Sertum laetitiae*, AAS 31 (1939) 635-644.

achieve efficiently, is a matter of great urgency. Such groups and societies must be considered absolutely essential for the safeguarding of man's personal freedom and dignity, while leaving intact a sense of responsibility.[21]

The Right to Emigrate and Immigrate

25. Again, every human being has the right to freedom of movement and of residence within the confines of his own State. When there are just reasons in favour of it, he must be permitted to emigrate to other countries and take up residence there.[22] The fact that he is a citizen of a particular State does not deprive him of membership in the human family, nor of citizenship in that universal society, the common, world-wide fellowship of men.

Political Rights

26. Finally, man's personal dignity involves his right to take an active part in public life, and to make his own contribution to the common welfare of his fellow citizens. As Pope Pius XII said, "man as such, far from being an object or, as it were, an inert element in society, is rather its subject, its basis and its purpose; and so must he be esteemed".[23]

27. As a human person he is entitled to the legal protection of his rights, and such protection must be effective, unbiased, and strictly just. To quote again Pope Pius XII: "In consequence of that juridical order willed by God, man has his own inalienable right to

[21] Cf. AAS 53 (1961) 430.
[22] Cf. Pius XII, Broadcast message, Christmas 1952, AAS 45 (1953) 36-46.
[23] Cf. Pius XII, Broadcast message, Christmas 1944, AAS 37 (1945) 12.

juridical security. To him is assigned a certain, well-defined sphere of law, immune from arbitrary attack".[24]

Duties

28. The natural rights of which We have so far been speaking are inextricably bound up with as many duties, all applying to one and the same person. These rights and duties derive their origin, their sustenance, and their indestructibility from the natural law, which in conferring the one imposes the other.

29. Thus, for example, the right to live involves the duty to preserve one's life; the right to a decent standard of living, the duty to live in a becoming fashion; the right to be free to seek out the truth, the duty to devote oneself to an ever deeper and wider search for it.

Reciprocity of Rights and Duties Between Persons

30. Once this is admitted, it follows that in human society one man's natural right gives rise to a corresponding duty in other men; the duty, that is, of recognising and respecting that right. Every basic human right draws its authoritative force from the natural law, which confers it and attaches to it its respective duty. Hence, to claim one's rights and ignore one's duties, or only half fulfill them, is like building a house with one hand and tearing it down with the other.

Mutual Collaboration

31. Since men are social by nature, they must live together and consult each other's interests. That men should recognise and perform their respective rights and duties is imperative to a well-ordered society. But the result will be that each individual will make his whole-hearted contribution to the creation of a civic

[24] Cf. Pius XII, Broadcast message, Christmas 1942, AAS 35 (1943) 21.

order in which rights and duties are ever more diligently and more effectively observed.

32. For example, it is useless to admit that a man has a right to the necessities of life, unless we also do all in our power to supply him with means sufficient for his livelihood.

33. Hence society must not only be well-ordered, it must also provide men with abundant resources. This postulates not only the mutual recognition and fulfillment of rights and duties, but also the involvement and collaboration of all men in the many enterprises which our present civilisation makes possible, encourages or indeed demands.

An Attitude of Responsibility

34. Man's personal dignity requires besides that he enjoy freedom and be able to make up his own mind when he acts. In his association with his fellows, therefore, there is every reason why his recognition of rights, observance of duties, and many-sided collaboration with other men, should be primarily a matter of his own personal decision. Each man should act on his own initiative, conviction, and sense of responsibility, not under the constant pressure of external coercion or enticement. There is nothing human about a society that is welded together by force. Far from encouraging, as it should, the attainment of man's progress and perfection, it is merely an obstacle to his freedom.

Social Life in Truth, Justice, Charity and Freedom

35. Hence, before a society can be considered well-ordered, creative, and consonant with human dignity, it must be based on truth. St. Paul expressed this as follows: "Putting away lying, speak ye the truth every man with his neighbour, for we are members one of

another".[25] And so will it be, if each man acknowledges sincerely his own rights and his own duties toward others.

Human society, as We here picture it, demands that men be guided by justice, respect the rights of others and do their duty. It demands, too, that they be animated by such love as will make them feel the needs of others as their own, and induce them to share their goods with others, and to strive in the world to make all men alike heirs to the noblest of intellectual and spiritual values. Nor is this enough; for human society thrives on freedom, namely, on the use of means which are consistent with the dignity of its individual members, who, being endowed with reason, assume responsibility for their own actions.

36. And so, dearest sons and brothers, We must think of human society as being primarily a spiritual reality. By its means enlightened men can share their knowledge of the truth, can claim their rights and fulfill their duties, receive encouragement in their aspirations for the goods of the spirit, share their enjoyment of all the wholesome pleasures of the world, and strive continually to pass on to others all that is best in themselves and to make their own the spiritual riches of others. It is these spiritual values which exert a guiding influence on culture, economics, social institutions, political movements and forms, laws, and all the other components which go to make up the external community of men and its continual development.

God and the Moral Order

37. Now the order which prevails in human society is wholly incorporeal in nature. Its foundation is truth, and it must be brought into effect by justice.

[25] *Eph* 4:25.

It needs to be animated and perfected by men's love for one another, and, while preserving freedom intact, it must make for an equilibrium in society which is increasingly more human in character.

38. But such an order — universal, absolute and immutable in its principles — finds its source in the true, personal and transcendent God. He is the first truth, the sovereign good, and as such the deepest source from which human society, if it is to be properly constituted, creative, and worthy of man's dignity, draws its genuine vitality.[26] This is what St. Thomas means when he says: "Human reason is the standard which measures the degree of goodness of the human will, and as such it derives from the eternal law, which is divine reason... Hence it is clear that the goodness of the human will depends much more on the eternal law than on human reason".[27]

Characteristics of the Present Day

39. There are three things which characterise our modern age.

40. In the first place we notice a progressive improvement in the economic and social condition of working men. They began by claiming their rights principally in the economic and social spheres, and then proceeded to lay claim to their political rights as well. Finally, they have turned their attention to acquiring the more cultural benefits of society.

Today, therefore, working men all over the world are loud in their demands that they shall in no circumstances be subjected to arbitrary treatment, as though devoid of intelligence and freedom. They insist on being

[26] Cf. Pius XII, Broadcast message, Christmas 1942, AAS 35 (1943) 14.
[27] *Summa Theol.* Ia-IIae, q. 19, a. 4; cf. a. 9.

treated as human beings, with a share in every sector of human society: in the socio-economic sphere, in government, and in the realm of learning and culture.

41.   Secondly, the part that women are now playing in political life is everywhere evident. This is a development that is perhaps of swifter growth among Christian nations, but it is also happening extensively, if more slowly, among nations that are heirs to different traditions and imbued with a different culture. Women are gaining an increasing awareness of their natural dignity. Far from being content with a purely passive role or allowing themselves to be regarded as a kind of instrument, they are demanding both in domestic and in public life the rights and duties which belong to them as human persons.

42.   Finally, we are confronted in this modern age with a form of society which is evolving on entirely new social and political lines. Since all peoples have either attained political independence or are on the way to attaining it, soon no nation will rule over another and none will be subject to an alien power.

43.   Thus all over the world men are either the citizens of an independent State, or are shortly to become so; nor is any nation nowadays content to submit to foreign domination. The longstanding inferiority complex of certain classes because of their economic and social status, sex, or position in the State, and the corresponding superiority complex of other classes, is rapidly becoming a thing of the past.

Equality of Men

44.   Today, on the contrary, the conviction is widespread that all men are equal in natural dignity; and so, on the doctrinal and theoretical level, at least, no form of approval is being given to racial discrimination. All this is of supreme significance for the for-

mation of a human society animated by the principles We have mentioned above, for man's awareness of his rights must inevitably lead him to the recognition of his duties. The possession of rights involves the duty of implementing those rights, for they are the expression of a man's personal dignity. And the possession of rights also involves their recognition and respect by other people.

45. When society is formed on a basis of rights and duties, men have an immediate grasp of spiritual and intellectual values, and have no difficulty in understanding what is meant by truth, justice, charity and freedom. They become, moreover, conscious of being members of such a society. And that is not all. Inspired by such principles, they attain to a better knowledge of the true God — a personal God transcending human nature. They recognise that their relationship with God forms the very foundation of their life — the interior life of the spirit, and the life which they live in the society of their fellows.

II. RELATIONS BETWEEN INDIVIDUALS AND THE PUBLIC AUTHORITIES

46. Human society can be neither well-ordered nor prosperous without the presence of those who, invested with legal authority, preserve its institutions and do all that is necessary to sponsor actively the interests of all its members. And they derive their authority from God, for, as St. Paul teaches, "there is no power but from God".[28]

In his commentary on this passage, St. John Chrysostom writes: "What are you saying? Is every ruler appointed by God? No, that is not what I mean, he says, for I am not now talking about individual rulers, but about authority as such. My contention is that the existence of a ruling authority — the fact that some should command and others obey, and that all things not come about as the result of blind chance — this is a provision of divine wisdom".[29]

God has created men social by nature, and a society cannot "hold together unless someone is in command to give effective direction and unity of purpose. Hence every civilised community must have a ruling authority, and this authority, no less than society itself, has its source in nature, and consequently has God for its author".[30]

47. But it must not be imagined that authority knows no bounds. Since its starting point is the per-

[28] *Rom* 13:1-6.
[29] *In Epist. ad Rom* c. 13, vv. 1-2, homil. XXIII; PG 60. 615.
[30] Leo XIII, Encyclical epistle *Immortale Dei*, Acta Leonis XIII, V, 1885, p. 120.

mission to govern in accordance with right reason, there is no escaping the conclusion that it derives its binding force from the moral order, which in turn has God as its origin and end.

Hence, to quote Pope Pius XII, "The absolute order of living beings, and the very purpose of man — an autonomous being, the subject of duties and inviolable rights, and the origin and purpose of human society — have a direct bearing upon the State as a necessary community endowed with authority. Divest it of this authority, and it is nothing, it is lifeless... But right reason, and above all Christian faith, make it clear that such an order can have no other origin but in God, a personal God, our Creator. Hence it is from Him that State officials derive their dignity, for they share to some extent in the authority of God Himself".[31]

An Appeal to Conscience

48.   Hence, a regime which governs solely or mainly by means of threats and intimidation or promises of reward, provides men with no effective incentive to work for the common good. And even if it did, it would certainly be offensive to the dignity of free and rational human beings. Authority is before all else a moral force. For this reason the appeal of rulers should be to the individual conscience, to the duty which every man has of voluntarily contributing to the common good. But since all men are equal in natural dignity, no man has the capacity to force internal compliance on another. Only God can do that, for He alone scrutinises and judges the secret counsels of the heart.

[31] Cf. Pius XII, Broadcast message, Christmas 1944, AAS 37 (1945) 15.

49.   Hence, representatives of the State have no power to bind men in conscience, unless their own authority is tied to God's authority, and is a participation in it.[32]

50.   The application of this principle likewise safeguards the dignity of citizens. Their obedience to civil authorities is never an obedience paid to them as men. It is in reality an act of homage paid to God, the provident Creator of the universe, who has decreed that men's dealings with one another be regulated in accordance with that order which He Himself has established. And we men do not demean ourselves in showing due reverence to God. On the contrary, we are lifted up and ennobled in spirit, for to serve God is to reign.[33]

51.   Governmental authority, therefore, is a postulate of the moral order and derives from God. Consequently, laws and decrees passed in contravention of the moral order, and hence of the divine will, can have no binding force in conscience, since "it is right to obey God rather than men".[34]

Indeed, the passing of such laws undermines the very nature of authority and results in shameful abuse. As St. Thomas teaches, "In regard to the second proposition, we maintain that human law has the rationale of law insofar as it is in accordance with right reason, and as such it obviously derives from eternal law. A law which is at variance with reason is to that extent unjust and has no longer the rationale of law. It is rather an act of violence".[35]

---

[32] Cf. Leo XIII, Encyclical epistle *Diuturnum illud*, Acta Leonis XIII, 11, 1881, p. 274.

[33] Cf. *ibid.*, p. 278; also Leo XIII, Encyclical epistle *Immortale Dei*, Acta Leonis XIII, V, 1885, p. 130.

[34] *Acts* 5:29.

[35] *Summa Theol.* Ia-IIae, q. 93, a. 3 ad 2um; cf. Pius XII, Broadcast message, Christmas 1945, AAS 37 (1945) 5-23.

52.   The fact that authority comes from God does not mean that men have no power to choose those who are to rule the State, or to decide upon the type of government they want, and determine the procedure and limitations of rulers in the exercise of their authority. Hence the above teaching is consonant with any genuinely democratic form of government.[36]

Attainment of the Common Good is the Purpose
of the Public Authority

53.   Men, both as individuals and as intermediate groups, are required to make their own specific contributions to the general welfare. The main consequence of this is that they must harmonise their own interests with the needs of others, and offer their goods and services as their rulers shall direct — assuming, of course, that justice is maintained and the authorities are acting within the limits of their competence. Those who have authority in the State must exercise that authority in a way which is not only morally irreproachable, but also best calculated to ensure or promote the State's welfare.

54.   The attainment of the common good is the sole reason for the existence of civil authorities. In working for the common good, therefore, the authorities must obviously respect its nature, and at the same time adjust their legislation to meet the requirements of the given situation.[37]

---

[36] Cf. Leo XIII, Encyclical epistle *Diuturnum illud*, Acta Leonis XIII, II, 1881, pp. 271-273; and Pius XII, Broadcast message, Christmas 1944, AAS 37 (1945) 5-23.

[37] Cf. Pius XII, Broadcast message, Christmas 1942, AAS 35 (1943) 13; and Leo XIII, Encyclical epistle *Immortale Dei*, Acta Leonis XIII, V, 1885, p. 120.

55.   Among the essential elements of the common good one must certainly include the various characteristics distinctive of each individual people.[38] But these by no means constitute the whole of it. For the common good, since it is intimately bound up with human nature, can never exist fully and completely unless the human person is taken into account at all times. Thus, attention must be paid to the basic nature of the common good and what it is that brings it about.[39]

56.   We must add, therefore, that it is in the nature of the common good that every single citizen has the right to share in it — although in different ways, depending on his tasks, merits and circumstances. Hence every civil authority must strive to promote the common good in the interest of all, without favouring any individual citizen or category of citizens. As Pope Leo XIII insisted: "The civil power must not be subservient to the advantage of any one individual, or of some few persons; inasmuch as it was established for the common good of all".[40]

Nevertheless, considerations of justice and equity can at times demand that those in power pay more attention to the weaker members of society, since these are at a disadvantage when it comes to defending their own rights and asserting their legitimate interests.[41]

---

[38] Cf. Pius XII, Encyclical letter *Summi Pontificatus*, AAS 31 (1939) 412-453.

[39] Cf. Pius XI, Encyclical letter *Mit brennender Sorge*, AAS 29 (1937) 159, and his Encyclical letter *Divini Redemptoris*, AAS 29 (1937) 65-106.

[40] Leo XIII, Encyclical letter *Immortale Dei*, Acta Leonis XIII, V, 1885, p. 121.

[41] Cf. Leo XIII, Encyclical letter *Rerum novarum*, Acta Leonis XIII, XI, 1891, pp. 133-134.

The Spiritual, Too

57. In this connection, We would draw the attention of Our own sons to the fact that the common good is something which affects the needs of the whole man, body and soul. That, then, is the sort of good which rulers of States must take suitable measure to ensure. They must respect the hierarchy of values, and aim at achieving the spiritual as well as the material prosperity of their subjects.[42]

58. These principles are clearly contained in that passage in Our encyclical *Mater et Magistra* where We emphasised that the common good "must take account of all those social conditions which favour the full development of human personality".[43]

59. Consisting, as he does, of body and immortal soul, man cannot in this mortal life satisfy his needs or attain perfect happiness. Thus, the measures that are taken to implement the common good must not jeopardise his eternal salvation; indeed, they must even help him to obtain it.[44]

Responsibilities of the Public Authority, and Rights and Duties of Individuals

60. It is generally accepted today that the common good is best safeguarded when personal rights and duties are guaranteed. The chief concern of civil authorities must therefore be to ensure that these rights are recognised, respected, co-ordinated, defended and promoted, and that each individual is enabled to perform his duties more easily. For "to safeguard the inviolable rights of the human person,

[42] Cf. Pius XII, Encyclical letter *Summi Pontificatus*, AAS 31 (1939) 433.

[43] AAS 53 (1961) 417.

[44] Cf. Pius XI, Encyclical letter *Quadragesimo anno*, AAS 23 (1931) 215.

and to facilitate the performance of his duties, is the principal duty of every public authority".[45]

61. Thus any government which refused to recognise human rights or acted in violation of them, would not only fail in its duty; its decrees would be wholly lacking in binding force.[46]

Reconciliation and Protection of Rights and Duties of Individuals

62. One of the principal duties of any government, moreover, is the suitable and adequate superintendence and co-ordination of men's respective rights in society. This must be done in such a way 1) that the exercise of their rights by certain citizens does not obstruct other citizens in the exercise of theirs; 2) that the individual, standing upon his own rights, does not impede others in the performance of their duties; 3) that the rights of all be effectively safeguarded, and completely restored if they have been violated.[47]

Duty of Promoting the Rights of Individuals

63. In addition, heads of States must make a positive contribution to the creation of an overall climate in which the individual can both safeguard his own rights and fulfill his duties, and can do so readily. For if there is one thing we have learned in the school of experience, it is surely this: that, in the modern world especially, political, economic and cultural inequities

[45] Cf. Pius XII, Broadcast message, Pentecost, June 1, 1941, AAS 33 (1941) 200.
[46] Cf. Pius XI, Encyclical letter *Mit brennender Sorge*, AAS 29 (1937) 159, and his Encyclical letter *Divini Redemptoris*, AAS 29 (1937) 79; and Pius XII, Broadcast message, Christmas 1942, AAS 35 (1943) 9-24.
[47] Cf. Pius XI, Encyclical letter *Divini Redemptoris*, AAS 29 (1937) 81; and Pius XII, Broadcast message, Christmas 1942, AAS 35 (1943) 9-24.

among citizens become more and more widespread when public authorities fail to take appropriate action in these spheres. And the consequence is that human rights and duties are thus rendered totally ineffective.

64. The public administration must therefore give considerable care and thought to the question of social as well economic progress, and to the development of essential services in keeping with the expansion of the productive system. Such services include road-building, transportation, communications, drinking-water, housing, medical care, ample facilities for the practice of religion, and aids to recreation. The government must also see to the provision of insurance facilities, to obviate any likelihood of a citizen's being unable to maintain a decent standard of living in the event of some misfortune, or greatly increased family responsibilities.

The government is also required to show no less energy and efficiency in the matter of providing opportunities for suitable employment, graded to the capacity of the workers. It must make sure that working men are paid a just and equitable wage, and are allowed a sense of responsibility in the industrial concerns for which they work. It must facilitate the formation of intermediate groups, so that the social life of the people may become more fruitful and less constrained. And finally, it must ensure that everyone has the means and opportunity of sharing as far as possible in cultural benefits.

Harmonious Relations Between Public Authority's
Two Forms of Intervention

65. The common welfare further demands that in their efforts to co-ordinate and protect, and their efforts to promote, the rights of citizens, the civil authorities preserve a delicate balance. An excessive

concern for the rights of any particular individuals or groups might well result in the principal advantages of the State being in effect monopolised by these citizens. Or again, the absurd situation can arise where the civil authorities, while taking measures to protect the rights of citizens, themselves stand in the way of the full exercise of these rights. "For this principle must always be retained: that however extensive and far-reaching the influence of the State on the economy may be, it must never be exerted to the extent of depriving the individual citizen of his freedom of action. It must rather augment his freedom, while effectively guaranteeing the protection of everyone's essential, personal rights".[48]

66.   And the same principle must be adopted by civil authorities in their various efforts to facilitate the exercise of rights and performance of duties in every department of social life.

Structure and Operation of the Public Authority

67.   For the rest, it is not possible to give a general ruling on the most suitable form of government, or the ways in which civil authorities can most effectively fulfill their legislative, administrative, and judicial functions.

68.   In determining what form a particular government shall take, and the way in which it shall function, a major consideration will be the prevailing circumstances and the condition of the people; and these are things which vary in different places and at different times.

We think, however, that it is in keeping with human nature for the State to be given a form which

[48] JOHN XXIII, Encyclical letter *Mater et Magistra*, AAS 53 (1961) 415.

embodies a threefold division of public office properly corresponding to the three main functions of public authority. In such a State a precise legal framework is provided, not only for the official functions of government, but also for the mutual relations between citizens and public officials. This will obviously afford sure protection to citizens, both in the safeguarding of their rights and in the fulfillment of their duties.

69.   If, however, this juridical and political structure is to realise its potential benefits, it is absolutely essential that public officials do their utmost to solve the problems that arise; and they must do so by using policies and techniques which it is within their competence to implement, and which suit the actual condition of the State. It is also essential that, despite constantly changing conditions, legislators never disregard the moral law or constitutional provision, nor act at variance with the exigencies of the common good. And as justice must be the guiding principle in the administration of the State, and executives must thoroughly understand the law and carefully weigh all attendant circumstances, so too in the courts: justice must be administered impartially, and judges must be wholly incorrupt and uninfluenced by the solicitations of interested parties. The good order of society also requires that individuals and subsidiary groups within the State be effectively protected by law in the affirmation of their rights and the performance of their duties, both in their relations with each other and with government officials.[49]

[49] Cf. Pius XII, Broadcast message, Christmas 1942, AAS 35 (1943) 21.

70. There can be no doubt that a State juridical system which conforms to the principles of justice and rightness, and corresponds to the degree of civic maturity evinced by the State in question, is highly conducive to the attainment of the common good.

71. And yet social life is so complex, varied and active in this modern age, that even a juridical system which has been established with great prudence and foresight often seems inadequate to the need.

72. Moreover, the relations of citizens with each other, of citizens and intermediate groups with public authorities, and the relations between public authorities of the same State, are sometimes seen to be of so ambiguous and explosive a nature, that they are not susceptible of being regulated by any hard and fast system of laws.

In such cases, if the authorities want to preserve the State's juridical system intact — in itself and in its application to specific cases — and if they want to minister to the principal needs of society, adapt the laws to the conditions of modern life and seek solutions to new problems, then it is essential that they have a clear idea of the nature and limits of their own legitimate spheres of action. Their calmness, integrity, clear sightedness and perseverance must be such that they will recognise at once what is needed in a given situation, and act with promptness and efficiency.[50]

Citizens' Participation in Public Life

73. A natural consequence of men's dignity is unquestionably their right to take an active part in government, though their degree of participation will

---

[50] Cf. PIUS XII, Broadcast message, Christmas 1944, AAS 37 (1945) 15-16.

necessarily depend on the stage of development reached by the political community of which they are members.

74.   For the rest, this right to take part in government opens out to men a new and extensive field of opportunity for service. A situation is created in which civic authorities can, from the greater frequency of their contacts and discussions with the citizens, gain a clearer idea of what policies are in fact effectual for the common good; and in a system which allows for a regular succession of public officials, the authority of these officials, far from growing old and feeble, takes on a new vitality in keeping with the progressive development of human society.[51]

Characteristics of the Present Day

75.   There is every indication at the present time that these aims and ideals are giving rise to various demands concerning the juridical organisation of States. The first is this: that a clear and precisely worded charter of fundamental human rights be formulated and incorporated into the State's general constitutions.

76.   Secondly, each State must have a public constitution, couched in juridical terms, laying down clear rules relating to the designation of public officials, their reciprocal relations, spheres of competence and prescribed methods of operation.

77.   The final demand is that relations between citizens and public authorities be described in terms of rights and duties. It must be clearly laid down that the principal function of public authorities is to recognise, respect, co-ordinate, safeguard and promote citizens' rights and duties.

[51] Cf. Pius XII, Broadcast message, Christmas 1942, AAS 35 (1943) 12.

78. We must, however, reject the view that the will of the individual or the group is the primary and only source of a citizen's rights and duties, and of the binding force of political constitutions and the government's authority.[52]

79. But the aspirations We have mentioned are a clear indication of the fact that men, increasingly aware nowadays of their personal dignity, have found the incentive to enter government service and demand constitutional recognition for their own inviolable rights. Not content with this, they are demanding, too, the observance of constitutional procedures in the appointment of public authorities, and are insisting that they exercise their office within this constitutional framework.

[52] Cf. LEO XIII, Apostolic letter *Annum ingressi*, Acta Leonis XIII, XXII, 1902-1903, pp. 52-80.

III. RELATIONS BETWEEN STATES

80. With respect to States themselves, Our predecessors have constantly taught, and We wish to lend the weight of Our own authority to their teaching, that nations are the subjects of reciprocal rights and duties. Their relationships, therefore, must likewise be harmonised in accordance with the dictates of truth, justice, willing co-operation, and freedom. The same law of nature that governs the life and conduct of individuals must also regulate the relations of political communities with one another.

81. This will be readily understood when one reflects that it is quite impossible for political leaders to lay aside their natural dignity while acting in their country's name and in its interests. They are still bound by the natural law, which is the rule that governs all moral conduct, and they have no authority to depart from its slightest precepts.

82. The idea that men, by the fact of their appointment to public office, are compelled to lay aside their own humanity, is quite inconceivable. Their very attainment to this high-ranking office was due to their exceptional gifts and intellectual qualities, which earned for them their reputation as outstanding representatives of the body politic.

83. Moreover, a ruling authority is indispensable to civil society. That is a fact which follows from the moral order itself. Such authority, therefore, cannot be misdirected against the moral order. It would immediately cease to exit, being deprived of its whole *raison d'être*. God Himself warns us of this: "Hear, therefore, ye kings, and understand: learn, ye that

are judges of the ends of the earth. Give ear, you that rule the people, and that please yourselves in multitudes of nations. For power is given you by the Lord, and strength by the Most High, who will examine your works, and search out your thoughts".[53]

84.   And lastly one must bear in mind that, even when it regulates the relations between States, authority must be exercised for the promotion of the common good. That is the primary reason for its existence.

An Imperative of the Common Good

85.   But one of the principal imperatives of the common good is the recognition of the moral order and the unfailing observance of its precepts. "A firmly established order between political communities must be founded on the unshakable and unmoving rock of the moral law, that law which is revealed in the order of nature by the Creator Himself, and engraved indelibly on men's hearts... Its principles are beacon lights to guide the policies of men and nations. They are also warning lights — providential signs — which men must heed if their laborious efforts to establish a new order are not to encounter perilous storms and shipwreck".[54]

In Truth

86.   The first point to be settled is that mutual ties between States must be governed by truth. Truth calls for the elimination of every trace of racial discrimination, and the consequent recognition of the inviolable principle that all States are by nature equal in dignity.

---

[53] *Wis* 6:1-4.
[54] Cf. Pius XII, Broadcast message, Christmas 1941, AAS 34 (1942) 16.

Each of them accordingly has the right to exist, to develop, and to possess the necessary means and accept a primary responsibility for its own development. Each is also legitimately entitled to its good name and to the respect which is its due.

87.   As we know from experience, men frequently differ widely in knowledge, virtue, intelligence and wealth, but that is no valid argument in favour of a system whereby those who are in a position of superiority impose their will arbitrarily on others. On the contrary, such men have a greater share in the common responsibility to help others to reach perfection by their mutual efforts.

88.   So, too, on the international level: some nations may have attained to a superior degree of scientific, cultural and economic development. But that does not entitle them to exert unjust political domination over other nations. It means that they have to make a greater contribution to the common cause of social progress.

89.   The fact is that no one can be by nature superior to his fellows, since all men are equally noble in natural dignity. And consequently there are no differences at all between political communities from the point of view of natural dignity. Each State is like a body, the members of which are human beings. And, as we know from experience, nations can be highly sensitive in matters in any way touching their dignity and honour; and with good reason.

The Question of Propaganda

90.   Truth further demands an attitude of unruffled impartiality in the use of the many aids to the promotion and spread of mutual understanding between nations which modern scientific progress has made available. This does not mean that people should be

prevented from drawing particular attention to the virtues of their own way of life, but it does mean the utter rejection of ways of disseminating information which violate the principles of truth and justice, and injure the reputation of another nation.[55]

In Justice

91.   Relations between States must furthermore be regulated by justice. This necessitates both the recognition of their mutual rights, and, at the same time, the fulfillment of their respective duties.

92.   States have the right to existence, to self-development, and to the means necessary to achieve this. They have the right to play the leading part in the process of their own development, and the right to their good name and due honours. Consequently, States are likewise in duty bound to safeguard all such rights effectively, and to avoid any action that could violate them. And just as individual men may not pursue their own private interests in a way that is unfair and detrimental to others, so too it would be criminal in a State to aim at improving itself by the use of methods which involve other nations in injury and unjust oppression. There is a saying of St. Augustine which has particular relevance in this context: "Take away justice, and what are kingdoms but mighty bands of robbers".[56]

93.   There may be, and sometimes is, a clash of interests among States, each striving for its own development. When differences of this sort arise, they must be settled in a truly human way, not by armed force nor by deceit or trickery. There must be a mu-

---

[55] Cf. Pius XII, Broadcast message, Christmas 1940, AAS 33 (1941) 5-14.

[56] *De civitate Dei*, lib. IV, c. 4; PL 41. 115; cf. Pius XII, Broadcast message, Christmas 1939, AAS 32 (1940) 5-13.

tual assessment of the arguments and feelings on both sides, a mature and objective investigation of the situation, and an equitable reconciliation of opposing views.

The Treatment of Minorities

94. A special instance of this clash of interests is furnished by that political trend (which since the nineteenth century has become widespread throughout the world and has gained in strength) as a result of which men of similar ethnic background are anxious for political autonomy and unification into a single nation. For many reasons this cannot always be effected, and consequently minority peoples are often obliged to live within the territories of a nation of a different ethnic origin. This situation gives rise to serious problems.

95. It is quite clear that any attempt to check the vitality and growth of these ethnic minorities is a flagrant violation of justice; the more so if such perverse efforts are aimed at their very extinction.

96. Indeed, the best interests of justice are served by those public authorities who do all they can to improve the human conditions of the members of these minority groups, especially in what concerns their language, culture, ancient traditions, and their economic activity and enterprise.[57]

A Cautionary Note

97. It is worth noting, however, that these minority groups, in reaction, perhaps, to the enforced hardships of their present situation, or to historical circumstances, frequently tend to magnify unduly char-

---

[57] Cf. Pius XII, Broadcast message, Christmas 1941, AAS 34 (1942) 10-21.

acteristics proper to their own people. They even rate them above those human values which are common to all mankind, as though the good of the entire human family should subserve the interests of their own particular groups. A more reasonable attitude for such people to adopt would be to recognise the advantages, too, which accrue to them from their own special situation. They should realise that their constant association with a people steeped in a different civilisation from their own has no small part to play in the development of their own particular genius and spirit. Little by little they can absorb into their very being those virtues which characterise the other nation. But for this to happen these minority groups must enter into some kind of association with the people in whose midst they are living, and learn to share their customs and way of life. It will never happen if they sow seeds of disaffection which can only produce a harvest of evils, stifling the political development of nations.

Active Solidarity

98. Since relationships between States must be regulated in accordance with the principles of truth and justice, States must further these relationships by taking positive steps to pool their material and spiritual resources. In many cases this can be achieved by all kinds of mutual collaboration; and this is already happening in our own day in the economic, social, political, educational, health and athletic spheres — and with beneficial results. We must bear in mind that of its very nature civil authority exists, not to confine men within the frontiers of their own nations, but primarily to protect the common good of the State, which certainly cannot be divorced from the common good of the entire human family.

99.   Thus, in pursuing their own interests, civil societies, far from causing injury to others, must join plans and forces whenever the efforts of particular States cannot achieve the desired goal. But in doing so great care must be taken. What is beneficial to some States may prove detrimental rather than advantageous to others.

Contacts Between Races

100.   Furthermore, the universal common good requires the encouragement in all nations of every kind of reciprocation between citizens and their intermediate societies. There are many parts of the world where we find groupings of people of more or less different ethnic origin. Nothing must be allowed to prevent reciprocal relations between them. Indeed such a prohibition would flout the very spirit of an age which has done so much to nullify the distances separating peoples.

Nor must one overlook the fact that whatever their ethnic background, men possess, besides the special characteristics which distinguish them from other men, other very important elements in common with the rest of mankind. And these can form the basis of their progressive development and self-realisation especially in regard to spiritual values. They have, therefore, the right and duty to carry on their lives with others in society.

The Proper Balance Between Population, Land and Capital

101.   As everyone is well aware, there are some countries where there is an imbalance between the amount of arable land and the number of inhabitants; others where there is an imbalance between the richness of the resources and the instruments of agriculture available. It is imperative, therefore, that nations

51

enter into collaboration with each other, and facilitate the circulation of goods, capital and manpower.[58]

102.   We advocate in such cases the policy of bringing the work to the workers, wherever possible, rather than bringing workers to the scene of the work. In this way many people will be afforded an opportunity of increasing their resources without being exposed to the painful necessity of uprooting themselves from their own homes, settling in a strange environment, and forming new social contacts.

The Problem of Political Refugees

103.   The deep feelings of paternal love for all mankind which God has implanted in Our heart makes it impossible for Us to view without bitter anguish of spirit the plight of those who for political reasons have been exiled from their own homelands. There are great numbers of such refugees at the present time, and many are the sufferings — the incredible sufferings — to which they are constantly exposed.

104.   Here surely is our proof that, in defining the scope of a just freedom within which individual citizens may live lives worthy of their human dignity, the rulers of some nations have been far too restrictive. Sometimes in States of this kind the very right to freedom is called in question, and even flatly denied. We have here a complete reversal of the right order of society, for the whole *raison d'être* of public authority is to safeguard the interests of the community. Its sovereign duty is to recognise the noble realm of freedom and protect its rights.

[58] Cf. JOHN XIII, Encyclical letter *Mater et Magistra*, AAS 53 (1961) 439.

The Refugee's Rights

105.   For this reason, it is not irrelevant to draw the attention of the world to the fact that these refugees are persons and all their rights as persons must be recognised. Refugees cannot lose these rights simply because they are deprived of citizenship of their own States.

106.   And among man's personal rights we must include his right to enter a country in which he hopes to be able to provide more fittingly for himself and his dependents. It is therefore the duty of State officials to accept such immigrants and — so far as the good of their own community, rightly understood, permits — to further the aims of those who may wish to become members of a new society.

Commendable Efforts

107.   We therefore take this opportunity of giving Our public approval and commendation to every undertaking, founded on the principles of human solidarity or of Christian charity, which aims at relieving the distress of those who are compelled to emigrate from their own country to another.

108.   And We must indeed single out for the praise of all right-minded men those international agencies which devote all their energies to this most important work.

Causes of the Arms Race

109.   On the other hand, We are deeply distressed to see the enormous stocks of armaments that have been, and continue to be, manufactured in the economically more developed countries. This policy is involving a vast outlay of intellectual and material resources, with the result that the people of these countries are saddled with a great burden, while other

countries lack the help they need for their economic and social development.

110.　There is a common belief that under modern conditions peace cannot be assured except on the basis of an equal balance of armaments and that this factor is the probable cause of this stockpiling of armaments. Thus, if one country increases its military strength, others are immediately roused by a competitive spirit to augment their own supply of armaments. And if one country is equipped with atomic weapons, others consider themselves justified in producing such weapons themselves, equal in destructive force.

111.　Consequently people are living in the grip of constant fear. They are afraid that at any moment the impending storm may break upon them with horrific violence. And they have good reasons for their fear, for there is certainly no lack of such weapons. While it is difficult to believe that anyone would dare to assume responsibility for initiating the appalling slaughter and destruction that war would bring in its wake, there is no denying that the conflagration could be started by some chance and unforeseen circumstance. Moreover, even though the monstrous power of modern weapons does indeed act as a deterrent, there is reason to fear that the very testing of nuclear devices for war purposes can, if continued, lead to serious danger for various forms of life on earth.

Need for Disarmament

112.　Hence justice, right reason, and the recognition of man's dignity cry out insistently for a cessation to the arms race. The stock-piles of armaments which have been built up in various countries must be reduced all round and simultaneously by the parties concerned. Nuclear weapons must be banned. A general agreement must be reached on a suitable disarmament program, with an effective system of mutual control. In the words of Pope Pius XII: "The calamity of a world war, with the economic and social ruin and the moral excesses and dissolution that accompany it, must not on any account be permitted to engulf the human race for a third time".[59]

113.   Everyone, however, must realise that, unless this process of disarmament be thoroughgoing and complete, and reach men's very souls, it is impossible to stop the arms race, or to reduce armaments, or — and this is the main thing — ultimately to abolish them entirely. Everyone must sincerely co-operate in the effort to banish fear and the anxious expectation of war from men's minds. But this requires that the fundamental principles upon which peace is based in today's world be replaced by an altogether different one, namely, the realisation that true and lasting peace among nations cannot consist in the possession of an equal supply of armaments but only in mutual trust. And We are confident that this can be achieved, for it is a thing which not only is dictated by common sense, but is in itself most desirable and most fruitful of good.

Three Motives

114.   Here, then, we have an objective dictated first of all by reason. There is general agreement — or at least there should be — that relations between States, as between individuals, must be regulated not by armed force, but in accordance with the principles

---

[59] Cf. Pius XII, Broadcast message, Christmas 1941, AAS 34 (1942) 17; and Benedict XV, Exhortation to the rulers of the belligerent powers, August 1, 1917, AAS 9 (1917) 418.

of right reason: the principles, that is, of truth, justice and vigorous and sincere co-operation.

115. Secondly, it is an objective which We maintain is more earnestly to be desired. For who is there who does not feel the craving to be rid of the threat of war, and to see peace preserved and made daily more secure?

116. And finally it is an objective which is rich with possibilities for good. Its advantages will be felt everywhere, by individuals, by families, by nations, by the whole human race. The warning of Pope Pius XII still rings in our ears: "Nothing is lost by peace; everything may be lost by war".[60]

A Call to Unsparing Effort

117. We therefore consider it Our duty as the vicar on earth of Jesus Christ — the Saviour of the world, the Author of peace — and as interpreter of the most ardent wishes of the whole human family, in the fatherly love We bear all mankind, to beg and beseech mankind, and above all the rulers of States, to be unsparing of their labour and efforts to ensure that human affairs follow a rational and dignified course.

118. In their deliberations together, let men of outstanding wisdom and influence give serious thought to the problem of achieving a more human adjustment of relations between States throughout the world. It must be an adjustment that is based on mutual trust, sincerity in negotiation, and the faithful fulfillment of obligations assumed. Every aspect of the problem must be examined, so that eventually there may emerge some point of agreement from which to initiate treaties which are sincere, lasting, and beneficial in their effects.

[60] Cf. Pius XII, Broadcast message, August 24, 1939, AAS 31 (1939) 334.

119.   We, for Our part, will pray unceasingly that God may bless these labours by His divine assistance, and make them fruitful.

In Liberty

120.   Furthermore, relations between States must be regulated by the principle of freedom. This means that no country has the right to take any action that would constitute an unjust oppression of other countries, or an unwarranted interference in their affairs. On the contrary, all should help to develop in others an increasing awareness of their duties, an adventurous and enterprising spirit, and the resolution to take the initiative for their own advancement in every field of endeavour.

The Evolution of Economically Under-developed Countries

121.   All men are united by their common origin and fellowship, their redemption by Christ, and their supernatural destiny. They are called to form one Christian family. In Our encyclical *Mater et Magistra*, therefore, We appealed to the more wealthy nations to render every kind of assistance to those States which are still in the process of economic development.[61]

122.   It is no small consolation to Us to be able to testify here to the wide acceptance of Our appeal, and We are confident that in the years that lie ahead it will be accepted even more widely. The result We look for is that the poorer States shall in as short a time as possible attain to a degree of economic development that enables their citizens to live in conditions more in keeping with their human dignity.

123.   Again and again We must insist on the need for helping these peoples in a way which guarantees to them the preservation of their own freedom. They must

[61]   AAS 53 (1961) 440-441.

be conscious that they are themselves playing the major role in their economic and social development; that they are themselves to shoulder the main burden of it.

124.   Hence the wisdom of Pope Pius XII's teaching: "A new order founded on moral principles is the surest bulwark against the violation of the freedom, integrity and security of other nations, no matter what may be their territorial extension or their capacity for defense. For although it is almost inevitable that the larger States, in view of their greater power and vaster resources, will themselves decide on the norms governing their economic associations with small States, nevertheless these smaller States cannot be denied their right, in keeping with the common good, to political freedom, and to the adoption of a position of neutrality in the conflicts between nations. No State can be denied this right, for it is a postulate of the natural law itself, as also of international law. These smaller States have also the right of assuring their own economic development. It is only with the effective guaranteeing of these rights that smaller nations can fittingly promote the common good of all mankind, as well as the material welfare and the cultural and spiritual progress of their own people".[62]

125.   The wealthier States, therefore, while providing various forms of assistance to the poorer, must have the highest possible respect for the latter's national characteristics and timehonoured civil institutions. They must also repudiate any policy of domination. If this can be achieved, then "a precious contribution will have been made to the formation of a world community, in which each individual nation, conscious of its rights and duties, can work on

[62] Cf. Pius XII, Broadcast message, Christmas 1941, AAS 34 (1942) 16-17.

terms of equality with the rest for the attainment of universal prosperity".[63]

Signs of the Times

126.   Men nowadays are becoming more and more convinced that any disputes which may arise between nations must be resolved by negotiation and agreement, and not by recourse to arms.

127.   We acknowledge that this conviction owes its origin chiefly to the terrifying destructive force of modern weapons. It arises from fear of the ghastly and catastrophic consequences of their use. Thus, in this age which boasts of its atomic power, it no longer makes sense to maintain that war is a fit instrument with which to repair the violation of justice.

128.   And yet, unhappily, we often find the law of fear reigning supreme among nations and causing them to spend enormous sums on armaments. Their object is not aggression, so they say — and there is no reason for disbelieving them — but to deter others from aggression.

129.   Nevertheless, We are hopeful that, by establishing contact with one another and by a policy of negotiation, nations will come to a better recognition of the natural ties that bind them together as men. We are hopeful, too, that they will come to a fairer realisation of one of the cardinal duties deriving from our common nature: namely, that love, not fear, must dominate the relationships between individuals and between nations. It is principally characteristic of love that it draws men together in all sorts of ways, sincerely united in the bonds of mind and matter; and this is a union from which countless blessings can flow.

[63] JOHN XXIII, Encyclical letter *Mater et Magistra*, AAS 53 (1961) 443.

IV. RELATIONSHIP OF MEN AND OF POLITICAL COMMUNITIES WITH THE WORLD COMMUNITY

130.   Recent progress in science and technology has had a profound influence on man's way of life. This progress is a spur to men all over the world to extend their collaboration and association with one another in these days when material resources, travel from one country to another, and technical information have so vastly increased. This has led to a phenomenal growth in relationships between individuals, families and inter-mediate associations belonging to the various nations, and between the public authorities of the various po-litical communities. There is also a growing economic interdependence between States. National economies are gradually becoming so interdependent that a kind of world economy is being born from the simultaneous integration of the economies of individual States. And finally, each country's social progress, order, security and peace are necessarily linked with the social progress, order, security and peace of every other country.

131.   From this it is clear that no State can fittingly pursue its own interests in isolation from the rest, nor, under such circumstances, can it develop itself as it should. The prosperity and progress of any State is in part consequence, and in part cause, of the prosperity and progress of all other States.

Inadequacy of Modern States to Ensure Universal Common Good

132.   No era will ever succeed in destroying the unity of the human family, for it consists of men who are all equal by virtue of their natural dignity.

Hence there will always be an imperative need — born of man's very nature — to promote in sufficient measure the universal common good; the good, that is, of the whole human family.

133. In the past rulers of States seem to have been able to make sufficient provision for the universal common good through the normal diplomatic channels, or by top-level meetings and discussions, treaties and agreements; by using, that is, the ways and means suggested by the natural law, the law of nations, or international law.

134. In our own day, however, mutual relationships between States have undergone a far reaching change. On the one hand, the universal common good gives rise to problems of the utmost gravity, complexity and urgency — especially as regards the preservation of the security and peace of the whole world. On the other hand, the rulers of individual nations, being all on an equal footing, largely fail in their efforts to achieve this, however much they multiply their meetings and their endeavours to discover more fitting instruments of justice. And this is no reflection on their sincerity and enterprise. It is merely that their authority is not sufficiently influential.

135. We are thus driven to the conclusion that the shape and structure of political life in the modern world, and the influence exercised by public authority in all the nations of the world are unequal to the task of promoting the common good of all peoples.

Connection Between the Common Good and Political Authority

136. Now, if one considers carefully the inner significance of the common good on the one hand, and the nature and function of public authority on the other, one cannot fail to see that there is an intrinsic connection between them. Public authority, as the

means of promoting the common good in civil society, is a postulate of the moral order. But the moral order likewise requires that this authority be effective in attaining its end. Hence the civil institutions in which such authority resides, becomes operative and promotes its ends, are endowed with a certain kind of structure and efficacy: a structure and efficacy which make such institutions capable of realising the common good by ways and means adequate to the changing historical conditions.

137. Today the universal common good presents us with problems which are world-wide in their dimensions; problems, therefore, which cannot be solved except by a public authority with power, organisation and means co-extensive with these problems, and with a world-wide sphere of activity. Consequently the moral order itself demands the establishment of some such general form of public authority.

Public Authority Instituted
by Common Consent and Not Imposed by Force

138. But this general authority equipped with world-wide power and adequate means for achieving the universal common good cannot be imposed by force. It must be set up with the consent of all nations. If its work is to be effective, it must operate with fairness, absolute impartiality, and with dedication to the common good of all peoples. The forcible imposition by the more powerful nations of a universal authority of this kind would inevitably arouse fears of its being used as an instrument to serve the interests of the few or to take the side of a single nation, and thus the influence and effectiveness of its activity would be undermined. For even though nations may differ widely in material progress and military

strength, they are very sensitive as regards their juridical equality and the excellence of their own way of life. They are right, therefore, in their reluctance to submit to an authority imposed by force, established without their co-operation, or not accepted of their own accord.

The Universal Common Good and Personal Rights

139. The common good of individual States is something that cannot be determined without reference to the human person, and the same is true of the common good of all States taken together. Hence the public authority of the world community must likewise have as its special aim the recognition, respect, safeguarding and promotion of the rights of the human person. This can be done by direct action, if need be, or by the creation throughout the world of the sort of conditions in which rulers of individual States can more easily carry out their specific functions.

The Principle of Subsidiarity

140. The same principle of subsidiarity which governs the relations between public authorities and individuals, families and intermediate societies in a single State, must also apply to the relations between the public authority of the world community and the public authorities of each political community. The special function of this universal authority must be to evaluate and find a solution to economic, social, political and cultural problems which affect the universal common good. These are problems which, because of their extreme gravity, vastness and urgency, must be considered too difficult for the rulers of individual States to solve with any degree of success.

141.   But it is no part of the duty of universal authority to limit the sphere of action of the public authority
of individual States, or to arrogate any of their functions to itself. On the contrary, its essential purpose is
to create world conditions in which the public authorities of each nation, its citizens and intermediate
groups, can carry out their tasks, fullfill their duties
and claim their rights with greater security.[64]

Modern Developments

142.   The United Nations Organisation (U.N.) was
established, as is well known, on June 26, 1945. To it
were subsequently added lesser organisations consisting of members nominated by the public authority of
the various nations and entrusted with highly important international functions in the economic, social,
cultural, educational and health fields. The United
Nations Organisation has the special aim of maintaining and strengthening peace between nations, and of
encouraging and assisting friendly relations between
them, based on the principles of equality, mutual
respect, and extensive co-operation in every field of
human endeavour.

143.   A clear proof of the farsightedness of this organisation is provided by the Universal Declaration of
Human Rights passed by the United Nations General
Assembly on December 10, 1948. The preamble of
this declaration affirms that the genuine recognition
and complete observance of all the rights and free-
doms outlined in the declaration is a goal to be sought
by all peoples and all nations.

144.   We are, of course, aware that some of the
points in the declaration did not meet with unquali-

---

[64] Cf. Pius XII, Address to Young Members of Italian
Catholic Action, Rome, Sept. 12, 1948, AAS 40 (1948) 412.

fied approval in some quarters; and there was justification for this. Nevertheless, We think the document should be considered a step in the right direction, an approach toward the establishment of a juridical and political ordering of the world community. It is a solemn recognition of the personal dignity of every human being; an assertion of everyone's right to be free to seek out the truth, to follow moral principles, discharge the duties imposed by justice, and lead a fully human life. It also recognised other rights connected with these.

145. It is therefore Our earnest wish that the United Nations Organisation may be able progressively to adapt its structure and methods of operation to the magnitude and nobility of its tasks. May the day be not long delayed when every human being can find in this organisation an effective safeguard of his personal rights; those rights, that is, which derive directly from his dignity as a human person, and which are therefore universal, inviolable and inalienable. This is all the more desirable in that men today are taking an ever more active part in the public life of their own nations, and in doing so they are showing an increased interest in the affairs of all peoples. They are becoming more and more conscious of being living members of the universal family of mankind.

V. PASTORAL EXHORTATIONS

146.   Here once more We exhort Our sons to take an active part in public life, and to work together for the benefit of the whole human race, as well as for their own political communities. It is vitally necessary for them to endeavour, in the light of Christian faith, and with love as their guide, to ensure that every institution, whether economic, social, cultural or political, be such as not to obstruct but rather to facilitate man's self betterment, both in the natural and in the supernatural order.

Scientific Competence, Technical Capacity and Professional Experience

147.   And yet, if they are to imbue civilisation with right ideals and Christian principles, it is not enough for Our sons to be illumined by the heavenly light of faith and to be fired with enthusiasm for a cause; they must involve themselves in the work of these institutions, and strive to influence them effectively from within.

148.   But in a culture and civilisation like our own, which is so remarkable for its scientific knowledge and its technical discoveries, clearly no one can insinuate himself into public life unless he be scientifically competent, technically capable, and skilled in the practice of his own profession.

Apostolate of a Trained Laity

149.   And yet even this must be reckoned insufficient to bring the relationships of daily life into conformity with a more human standard, based, as it

must be, on truth, tempered by justice, motivated by mutual love, and holding fast to the practice of freedom.

150.   If these policies are really to become operative, men must first of all take the utmost care to conduct their various temporal activities in accordance with the laws which govern each and every such activity, observing the principles which correspond to their respective natures. Secondly, men's actions must be made to conform with the precepts of the moral order. This means that their behaviour must be such as to reflect their consciousness of exercising a personal right or performing a personal duty. Reason has a further demand to make. In obedience to the providential designs and commands of God respecting our salvation and neglecting the dictates of conscience, men must conduct themselves in their temporal activity in such a way as to effect a thorough integration of the principal spiritual values with those of science, technology and the professions.

Integration of Faith and Action

151.   In traditionally Christian States at the present time, civil institutions evince a high degree of scientific and technical progress and possess abundant machinery for the attainment of every kind of objective. And yet it must be owned that these institutions are often but slightly affected by Christian motives and a Christian spirit.

152.   One may well ask the reason for this, since the men who have largely contributed — and who are still contributing — to the creation of these institutions are men who are professed Christians, and who live their lives, at least in part, in accordance with the precepts of the gospels. In Our opinion the explanation lies in a certain cleavage between faith and prac-

tice. Their inner, spiritual unity must be restored, so that faith may be the light and love the motivating force of all their actions.

Integral Education

153.   We consider too that a further reason for this very frequent divorce between faith and practice in Christians is an inadequate education in Christian teaching and Christian morality. In many places the amount of energy devoted to the study of secular subjects is all too often out of proportion to that devoted to the study of religion. Scientific training reaches a very high level, whereas religious training generally does not advance beyond the elementary stage. It is essential, therefore, that the instruction given to our young people be complete and continuous, and imparted in such a way that moral goodness and the cultivation of religious values may keep pace with scientific knowledge and continually advancing technical progress. Young people must also be taught how to carry out their own particular obligations in a truly fitting manner.[65]

Constant Endeavour

154.   In this connection We think it opportune to point out how difficult it is to understand clearly the relation between the objective requirements of justice and concrete situations; to define, that is, correctly to what degree and in what form doctrinal principles and directives must be applied in the given state of human society.

155.   The definition of these degrees and forms is all the more difficult in an age such as ours, driven forward by a fever of activity. And yet this is the age in

[65] Cf. JOHN XXIII, Encyclical letter *Mater et Magistra*, AAS 53 (1961) 454.

which each one of us is required to make his own contribution to the universal common good. Daily is borne in on us the need to make the reality of social life conform better to the requirements of justice. Hence Our sons have every reason for not thinking that they can relax their efforts and be satisfied with what they have already achieved.

156.　What has so far been achieved is insufficient compared with what needs to be done; all men must realise that. Every day provides a more important, a more fitting enterprise to which they must turn their hands — industry, trade unions, professional organisations, insurance, cultural institutions, the law, politics, medical and recreational facilities, and other such activities. The age in which we live needs all these things. It is an age in which men, having discovered the atom and achieved the breakthrough into outer space, are now exploring other avenues, leading to almost limitless horizons.

Relations Between Catholics and Non-Catholics in Social and Economic Affairs

157.　The principles We have set out in this document take their rise from the very nature of things. They derive, for the most part, from the consideration of man's natural rights. Thus the putting of these principles into effect frequently involves extensive co-operation between Catholics and those Christians who are separated from this Apostolic See. It even involves the cooperation of Catholics with men who may not be Christians but who nevertheless are reasonable men, and men of natural moral integrity. "In such circumstances they must, of course, bear themselves as Catholics, and do nothing to compromise religion and morality. Yet at the same time they should show themselves animated by a spirit of understanding and unselfishness, ready to co-operate loyally in achieving objects which are good in themselves, or conducive to good".[66]

Error and the Errant

158.   It is always perfectly justifiable to distinguish between error as such and the person who falls into error — even in the case of men who err regarding the truth or are led astray as a result of their inadequate knowledge, in matters either of religion or of the highest ethical standards. A man who has fallen into error does not cease to be a man. He never forfeits his personal dignity; and that is something that must always be taken into account. Besides, there exists in man's very nature an undying capacity to break through the barriers of error and seek the road to truth. God, in His great providence, is ever present with His aid. Today, maybe, a man lacks faith and turns aside into error; tomorrow, perhaps, illumined by God's light, he may indeed embrace the truth.

Catholics who, in order to achieve some external good, collaborate with unbelievers or with those who through error lack the fullness of faith in Christ, may possibly provide the occasion or even the incentive for their conversion to the truth.

Philosophies and Historical Movements

159.   Again it is perfectly legitimate to make a clear distinction between a false philosophy of the nature, origin and purpose of men and the world, and economic, social, cultural, and political undertakings, even when such undertakings draw their origin and inspiration from that philosophy. True, the philosophic formula does not change once it has been set down in precise terms, but the undertakings

---

[66] *Ibid.*, p. 456.

clearly cannot avoid being influenced to a certain extent by the changing conditions in which they have to operate. Besides, who can deny the possible existence of good and commendable elements in these undertakings, elements which do indeed conform to the dictates of right reason, and are an expression of man's lawful aspirations?

160. It may sometimes happen, therefore, that meetings arranged for some practical end — though hitherto they were thought to be altogether useless — may in fact be fruitful at the present time, or at least offer prospects of success. But whether or not the moment for such co-operation has arrived, and the manner and degree of such co-operation in the attainment of economic, social, cultural and political advantages — these are matters for prudence to decide; prudence, the queen of all the virtues which rule the lives of men both as individuals and in society.

As far as Catholics are concerned, the decision rests primarily with those who take a leading part in the life of the community, and in these specific fields. They must, however, act in accordance with the principles of the natural law, and observe the Church's social teaching and the directives of ecclesiastical authority. For it must not be forgotten that the Church has the right and duty not only to safeguard her teaching on faith and morals, but also to exercise her authority over her sons by intervening in their external affairs whenever a judgment has to be made concerning the practical application of this teaching.[67]

---

[67] *Ibid.*, p. 456; cf. LEO XIII, Encyclical epistle *Immortale Dei*, Acta Leonis XIII, V, 1885, p. 128; PIUS XI, Encyclical letter *Ubi arcano*, AAS 14 (1922) 698; and PIUS XII, Address to the Union of International Sodalities of Catholic Women, Rome, Sept. 11, 1947, AAS 39 (1947) 486. AAS 39 (1947) 486.

Little by Little

161.   There are indeed some people who, in their generosity of spirit, burn with a desire to institute wholesale reforms whenever they come across situations which show scant regard for justice or are wholly out of keeping with its claims. They tackle the problem with such impetuosity that one would think they were embarking on some political revolution.

162.   We would remind such people that it is the law of nature that all things must be of gradual growth. If there is to be any improvement in human institutions, the work must be done slowly and deliberately from within. Pope Pius XII expressed it in these terms: "Salvation and justice consist not in the uprooting of an outdated system, but in a well-designed policy of development. Hot-headedness was never constructive; it has always destroyed everything. It has inflamed passions, but never assuaged them. It sows no seeds but those of hatred and destruction. Far from bringing about the reconciliation of contending parties, it reduces men and political parties to the necessity of laboriously redoing the work of the past, building on the ruins that disharmony has left in its wake". [68]

An Immense Task

163.   Hence among the very serious obligations incumbent upon men of high principles, We must include the task of establishing new relationships in human society, under the mastery and guidance of truth, justice, charity and freedom — relations between individual citizens, between citizens and their

[68] Cf. Pius XII, Address to Italian workers, Rome, Pentecost, June 13, 1943, AAS 35 (1943) 175.

respective States, between States, and finally between individuals, families, intermediate associations and States on the one hand, and the world community on the other. There is surely no one who will not consider this a most exalted task, for it is one which is able to bring about true peace in accordance with divinely established order.

164. Considering the need, the men who are shouldering this responsibility are far too few in number, yet they are deserving of the highest recognition from society, and We rightfully honour them with Our public praise. We call upon them to persevere in their ideals, which are of such tremendous benefit to mankind. At the same time We are encouraged to hope that many more men, Christians especially, will join their cause, spurred on by love and the realisation of their duty. Everyone who has joined the ranks of Christ must be a glowing point of light in the world, a nucleus of love, a leaven of the whole mass. He will be so in proportion to his degree of spiritual union with God.

165. The world will never be the dwellingplace of peace, till peace has found a home in the heart of each and every man, till every man preserves in himself the order ordained by God to be preserved. That is why St. Augustine asks the question: "Does your mind desire the strength to gain the mastery over your passions? Let it submit to a greater power, and it will conquer all beneath it. And peace will be in you — true, sure, most ordered peace. What is that order? God as ruler of the mind; the mind as ruler of the body. Nothing could be more orderly".[69]

[69] *Miscellanea Augustiniana...* St. Augustine, *Sermones post Maurinos reperti*, Rome, 1930, p. 633.

166. Our concern here has been with problems which are causing men extreme anxiety at the present time; problems which are intimately bound up with the progress of human society. Unquestionably, the teaching We have given has been inspired by a longing which We feel most keenly, and which We know is shared by all men of good will: that peace may be assured on earth.

167. We who, in spite of Our inadequacy, are nevertheless the vicar of Him whom the prophet announced as the Prince of Peace,[70] conceive of it as Our duty to devote all Our thoughts and care and energy to further this common good of all mankind. Yet peace is but an empty word, if it does not rest upon that order which Our hope prevailed upon Us to set forth in outline in this encyclical. It is an order that is founded on truth, built up on justice, nurtured and animated by charity, and brought into effect under the auspices of freedom.

168. So magnificent, so exalted is this aim that human resources alone, even though inspired by the most praiseworthy good will, cannot hope to achieve it. God Himself must come to man's aid with His heavenly assistance, if human society is to bear the closest possible resemblance to the kingdom of God.

169. The very order of things, therefore, demands that during this sacred season we pray earnestly to Him who by His bitter passion and death washed away men's sins, which are the fountainhead of discord, misery and inequality; to Him who shed His blood to reconcile the human race to the heavenly Father, and bestowed the gifts of peace. "For He is

[70] Cf. *Is* 9:6.

our peace, who hath made both one... And coming, He preached peace to you that were afar off; and peace to them that were nigh".[71]

170.   The sacred liturgy of these days reechoes the same message: "Our Lord Jesus Christ, after His resurrection stood in the midst of His disciples and said: Peace be upon you, alleluia. The disciples rejoiced when they saw the Lord".[72] It is Christ, therefore, who brought us peace; Christ who bequeathed it to us: "Peace I leave with you: my peace I give unto you: not as the world giveth, do I give unto you".[73]

171.   Let us, then, pray with all fervour for this peace which our divine Redeemer came to bring us. May He banish from the souls of men whatever might endanger peace. May He transform all men into witnesses of truth, justice and brotherly love. May He illumine with His light the minds of rulers, so that, besides caring for the proper material welfare of their peoples, they may also guarantee them the fairest gift of peace.

Finally, may Christ inflame the desires of all men to break through the barriers which divide them, to strengthen the bonds of mutual love, to learn to understand one another, and to pardon those who have done them wrong. Through His power and inspiration may all peoples welcome each other to their hearts as brothers, and may the peace they long for ever flower and ever reign among them.

172.   And so, dear brothers, with the ardent wish that peace may come upon the flocks committed to your care, for the special benefit of those who are

[71] *Eph* 2:14-17.
[72] Responsory at Matins, Feria VI within the Octave of Easter.
[73] *John* 14:27

most lowly and in the greatest need of help and defense, lovingly in the Lord We bestow on you, on Our priests both secular and regular, on religious both men and women, on all the faithful and especially those who give wholehearted obedience to these Our exhortations, Our Apostolic Blessing. And upon all men of good will, to whom We also address this encyclical, We implore from God health and prosperity.

Given at Rome, at St. Peter's, on Holy Thursday, the eleventh day of April, in the year 1963, the fifth of Our Pontificate.

JOHN XXIII

MESSAGE
OF HIS HOLINESS
POPE JOHN PAUL II
FOR THE CELEBRATION OF THE
WORLD DAY OF PEACE 2003

1. Almost forty years ago, on Holy Thursday, 11 April 1963, Pope John XXIII published his epic Encyclical Letter *Pacem in Terris*. Addressing himself to "all men of good will", my venerable predecessor, who would die just two months later, summed up his message of "peace on earth" in the first sentence of the Encyclical: "Peace on earth, which all men of every era have most eagerly yearned for, can be firmly established and sustained only if the order laid down by God be dutifully observed" (*Introduction: AAS*, 55 [1963], 257).

Speaking peace to a divided world

2. The world to which John XXIII wrote was then in a profound state of disorder. The twentieth century had begun with great expectations for progress. Yet within sixty years, that same century had produced two World Wars, devastating totalitarian systems, untold human suffering, and the greatest persecution of the Church in history.

Only two years before *Pacem in Terris*, in 1961, the Berlin Wall had been erected in order to divide and set against each other not only two parts of that City but two ways of understanding and building the earthly city. On one side and the other of the Wall, life was to follow different patterns, dictated by antithetical rules, in a climate of mutual suspicion and mistrust. Both as a world-view and in real life, that Wall traversed the whole of humanity and penetrated people's hearts and minds, creating divisions that seemed destined to last indefinitely.

Moreover, just six months before the Encyclical, and just as the Second Vatican Council was opening in Rome, the world had come to the brink of a nuclear war during the Cuban Missile Crisis. The road to a world of peace, justice and freedom seemed blocked. Humanity, many believed, was condemned to live indefinitely in that precarious condition of "cold war", hoping against hope that neither an act of aggression nor an accident would trigger the worst war in human history. Available atomic arsenals meant that such a war would have imperiled the very future of the human race.

The four pillars of peace

3.   Pope John XXIII did not agree with those who claimed that peace was impossible. With his Encyclical, *peace* — in all its demanding truth — came knocking on both sides of the Wall and of all the other dividing walls. The Encyclical spoke to everyone of their belonging to the one human family, and shone a light on the shared aspiration of people everywhere to live in security, justice and hope for the future.

With the profound intuition that characterized him, John XXIII identified the essential conditions for peace in four precise requirements of the human spirit: *truth, justice, love* and *freedom* (cf. *ibid.*, I: *l.c.*, 265-266). *Truth* will build peace if every individual sincerely acknowledges not only his rights, but also his own duties towards others. *Justice* will build peace if in practice everyone respects the rights of others and actually fulfils his duties towards them. *Love* will build peace if people feel the needs of others as their own and share what they have with others, especially the values of mind and spirit which they possess. *Freedom* will build peace and make it thrive if, in the choice of the means to that end, people act according to reason and assume responsibility for their own actions.

Looking at the present and into the future with the eyes of faith and reason, Blessed John XXIII discerned deeper historical currents at work. Things were not always what they seemed on the surface. Despite wars and rumours of wars, something more was at work in human affairs, something that to the Pope looked like the promising beginning of a spiritual revolution.

A new awareness of human dignity
and inalienable human rights

4.   Humanity, John XXIII wrote, had entered a new stage of its journey (cf. *ibid.*, I: *l.c.*, 267-269). The end of colonialism and the rise of newly independent States, the protection of workers' rights, the new and welcome presence of women in public life, all testified to the fact that the human race was indeed entering a new phase of its history, one characterized by *"the conviction that all men are equal by reason of their natural dignity"* (*ibid.*, I: *l.c.*, 268). The Pope knew that that dignity was still being trampled upon in many parts of the world. Yet he was convinced that, despite the dramatic situation, the world was becoming increasingly *conscious of certain spiritual values*, and increasingly open to the meaning of those *pillars of peace* — truth, justice, love, and freedom (cf. *ibid.*, I: *l.c.*, 268-269). Seeking to bring these values into local, national and international life, men and women were becoming more aware that their relationship with God, the source of all good, must be the solid foundation and supreme criterion of their lives, as individuals and in society (cf. *ibid.*). This evolving spiritual intuition would, the Pope was convinced, have profound public and political consequences.

Seeing the growth of awareness of human rights that was then emerging within nations and at the international level, Pope John XXIII caught the potential of this phenomenon and understood its singular power to change history. What was later to happen in central and eastern Europe would confirm his insight. The road to peace, he taught in the Encyclical, lay in the defence and promotion of basic human rights, which every human being enjoys, not as a benefit given by a different social class or conceded by the State but simply because of our humanity: "Any human society, if it is to be well-ordered and productive, must lay down as a foundation this principle, namely, that every human being is a person, that is, his nature is endowed with intelligence and free will. Indeed, precisely because he is a person he has rights and obligations, flowing directly and simultaneously from his very nature. And as these rights and obligations are universal and inviolable so they cannot in any way be surrendered" (*ibid.*, 259).

As history would soon show, this was not simply an abstract idea; it was an idea with profound consequences. Inspired by the conviction that every human being is equal in dignity, and that society therefore had to adapt its form to that conviction, *human rights movements* soon arose and gave concrete political expression to one of the great dynamics of contemporary history: the quest for freedom as an indispensable component of work for peace. Emerging in virtually every part of the world, these movements were instrumental in replacing dictatorial forms of government with more democratic and participatory ones. They demonstrated in practice that peace and progress could only be achieved by respecting *the universal moral law written on the human heart* (cf. JOHN PAUL II, *Address to the United Nations General Assembly*, 5 October 1995, No. 3).

5.   On another point too *Pacem in Terris* showed itself prophetic, as it looked to the next phase of the evolution of world politics. Because the world was becoming increasingly interdependent and global, the common good of humanity had to be worked out on the international plane. It was proper, Pope John XXIII taught, to speak of a *"universal common good"* (*Pacem in Terris,* IV: *l.c.,* 292). One of the consequences of this evolution was the obvious need for *a public authority, on the international level,* with effective capacity to advance the universal common good; an authority which could not, the Pope immediately continued, be established by coercion but only by the consent of nations. Such a body would have to have as its fundamental objective the "recognition, respect, safeguarding, and promotion of the rights of the human person" (*ibid.,* IV: *l.c.,* 294).

Not surprisingly therefore John XXIII looked with hope and expectation to the United Nations Organization, which had come into being on June 26, 1945. He saw that Organization as a credible instrument for maintaining and strengthening world peace, and he expressed particular appreciation of its 1948 *Universal Declaration of Human Rights*, which he considered "an approximation towards the establishment of a juridical and political organization of the world community" (*ibid.,* IV: *l.c.,* 295). What he was saying in fact was that the *Declaration* set out the moral foundations on which the evolution of a world characterized by order rather than disorder, and by dialogue rather than force, could proceed. He was suggesting that the vigorous defence of human rights by the United Nations Organization is the indispensable foundation for the development of that Organization's capacity to promote and defend international security.

Not only is it clear that Pope John XXIII's vision of an effective international public authority at the service of human rights, freedom and peace has not yet been entirely achieved, but there is still in fact much hesitation in the international community about the obligation to respect and implement human rights. This duty touches *all* fundamental rights, excluding that arbitrary picking and choosing which can lead to rationalizing forms of discrimination and injustice. Likewise, we are witnessing the emergence of an alarming gap between a series of new "rights" being promoted in advanced societies — the result of new prosperity and new technologies — and other more basic human rights still not being met, especially in situations of underdevelopment. I am thinking here for example about the right to food and drinkable water, to housing and security, to self-determination and independence — which are still far from being guaranteed and realized. *Peace demands that this tension be speedily reduced and in time eliminated.*

Another observation needs to be made: the international community, which since 1948 has possessed a charter of the inalienable rights of the human person, has generally failed to *insist sufficiently on corresponding duties.* It is *duty* that establishes the limits within which *rights* must be contained in order not to become an exercise in arbitrariness. A greater awareness of *universal human duties* would greatly benefit the cause of peace, setting it on the moral basis of a shared recognition of *an order in things* which is not dependent on the will of any individual or group.

6.   Nevertheless it remains true that, despite many difficulties and setbacks, *significant progress has been made* over the past forty years towards the implementation of Pope John's noble vision. The fact that States throughout the world feel obliged to honour the idea of human rights shows how powerful are the tools of moral conviction and spiritual integrity, which proved so decisive in the revolution of conscience that made possible the 1989 non-violent revolution that displaced European communism. And although distorted notions of freedom as licence continue to threaten democracy and free societies, it is surely significant that, in the forty years since *Pacem in Terris*, much of the world has become more free, structures of dialogue and cooperation between nations have been strengthened, and the threat of a global nuclear war, which weighed so heavily on Pope John XXIII, has been effectively contained.

Boldly, but with all humility, I would like to suggest that the Church's fifteen-hundred-year-old teaching on peace as *"tranquillitas ordinis* — the tranquillity of order" as Saint Augustine called it (*De Civitate Dei*, 19, 13), which was brought to a new level of development forty years ago by *Pacem in Terris,* has a deep relevance for the world today, for the leaders of nations as well as for individuals. That there is serious disorder in world affairs is obvious. Thus the question to be faced remains: *What kind of order can replace this disorder,* so that men and women can live in freedom, justice, and security? And since the world, amid its disorder, continues nevertheless to be "ordered" and organized in various ways — economic, cultural, even political — there arises another equally urgent question: On what principles are these new forms of world order unfolding?

These far-reaching questions suggest that the problem of order in world affairs, which is the problem of peace rightly understood, cannot be separated from issues of moral principle. This is another way of saying that the question of peace cannot be separated from the question of human dignity and human rights. That is one of the enduring truths taught by *Pacem in Terris*, which we would do well to remember and reflect upon on this fortieth anniversary.

Is this not the time for all to *work together for a new constitutional organization of the human family,* truly capable of ensuring peace and harmony between peoples, as well as their integral development? But let there be no misunderstanding. This does not mean writing the constitution of a global super-State. Rather, it means continuing and deepening processes already in place to meet the almost universal *demand for participatory ways of exercising political authority, even international political authority, and for transparency and accountability at every level of public life.* With his confidence in the goodness he believed could be found in every human person, Pope John XXIII called the entire world to a nobler vision of public life and public authority, even as he boldly challenged the world to think beyond its present state of disorder to new forms of international order commensurate with human dignity.

The bond between peace and truth

7.   Against those who think of politics as a realm of necessity detached from morality and subject only to partisan interests, Pope John XXIII, in *Pacem in Terris*, outlined a truer picture of human reality and indicated the path to a better future for all. Precisely because human beings are created with the capacity for moral choice, *no human activity takes place outside the sphere of moral judgment.* Politics is a human activity; therefore, it

too is subject to a distinctive form of moral scrutiny. This is also true of international politics. As the Pope wrote: "The same natural law that governs the life and conduct of individuals must also regulate the relations of political communities with one another" (*Pacem in Terris,* III: *l.c.,* 279). Those who imagine that international public life takes place somewhere outside the realm of moral judgment need only reflect on the impact of *human rights movements* on the national and international politics of the twentieth century just concluded. These developments, anticipated by the teaching of the Encyclical, decisively refute the claim that international politics must of necessity be a "free zone" in which the moral law holds no sway.

Perhaps nowhere today is there a more obvious need for the correct use of political authority than in *the dramatic situation of the Middle East and the Holy Land.* Day after day, year after year, the cumulative effect of bitter mutual rejection and an unending chain of violence and retaliation have shattered every effort so far to engage in serious dialogue on the real issues involved. The volatility of the situation is compounded by the clash of interests among the members of the international community. Until those in positions of responsibility undergo a veritable revolution in the way they use their power and go about securing their peoples' welfare, it is difficult to imagine how progress towards peace can be made. The fratricidal struggle that daily convulses the Holy Land and brings into conflict the forces shaping the immediate future of the Middle East shows clearly the need for men and women who, out of conviction, will implement policies firmly based on the principle of respect for human dignity and human rights. Such policies are incomparably more advantageous to everyone than the continuation of conflict. A start can be made on the

87

basis of this truth, which is certainly more liberating than propaganda, especially when that propaganda serves to conceal inadmissible intentions.

The premises of a lasting peace

8.   There is an unbreakable bond between *the work of peace* and *respect for truth*. Honesty in the supply of information, equity in legal systems, openness in democratic procedures give citizens a sense of security, a readiness to settle controversies by peaceful means, and a desire for genuine and constructive dialogue, all of which constitute *the true premises of a lasting peace*. Political summits on the regional and international levels serve the cause of peace only if joint commitments are then honoured by each party. Otherwise these meetings risk becoming irrelevant and useless, with the result that people believe less and less in dialogue and trust more in the use of force as a way of resolving issues. The negative repercussions on peace resulting from commitments made and then not honoured must be carefully assessed by State and government leaders.

Pacta sunt servanda, says the ancient maxim. If at all times commitments ought to be kept, *promises made to the poor* should be considered particularly binding. Especially frustrating for them is any breach of faith regarding promises which they see as vital to their well-being. In this respect, the failure to keep commitments in the sphere of aid to developing nations is a serious moral question and further highlights the injustice of the imbalances existing in the world. *The suffering caused by poverty is compounded by the loss of trust*. The end result is hopelessness. The existence of trust in international relations is *a social capital of fundamental value*.

A culture of peace

9.   In the end, peace is not essentially about *structures* but about *people*. Certain structures and mechanisms of peace — juridical, political, economic — are of course necessary and do exist, but they have been derived from nothing other than the accumulated wisdom and experience of *innumerable gestures of peace* made by men and women throughout history who have kept hope and have not given in to discouragement. *Gestures of peace* spring from the lives of people who *foster peace first of all in their own hearts*. They are the work of the heart and of reason in those who are peacemakers (cf. *Mt* 5:9). *Gestures of peace* are possible when people *appreciate fully the community dimension of their lives*, so that they grasp the meaning and consequences of events in their own communities and in the world. *Gestures of peace* create a tradition and a culture of peace.

   Religion has a vital role in fostering gestures of peace and in consolidating conditions for peace. It exercises this role all the more effectively if it concentrates on what is proper to it: attention to God, the fostering of universal brotherhood and the spreading of a culture of human solidarity. The *Day of Prayer for Peace* which I promoted in Assisi on 24 January 2002, involving representatives of many religions, had this purpose. It expressed a desire to nurture peace by spreading a spirituality and a culture of peace.

The legacy of Pacem in Terris

10.   Blessed Pope John XXIII was a man unafraid of the future. He was sustained in his optimism by his deep trust in God and in man, both of which grew out of the sturdy climate of faith in which he had grown up. Moved by his trust in Providence, even in what seemed like a permanent situation of conflict, he

did not hesitate to summon the leaders of his time to a new vision of the world. This is the legacy that he left us. On this World Day of Peace 2003, let us all resolve to have his same outlook: trust in the merciful and compassionate God who calls us to brotherhood, and confidence in the men and women of our time because, like those of every other time, they bear the image of God in their souls. It is on this basis that we can hope to build a world of peace on earth.

At the beginning of a new year in our human history, this is the hope that rises spontaneously from the depths of my heart: that in the spirit of every individual there may be a renewed dedication to the noble mission which *Pacem in Terris* proposed forty years ago to all men and women of good will. The task, which the Encyclical called "immense", is that "of establishing new relationships in human society, under the sway and guidance of truth, justice, love, and freedom". Pope John indicated that he was referring to "relations between individual citizens, between citizens and their respective States, between States, and finally between individuals, families, intermediate associations and States on the one hand, and the world community on the other". He concluded by saying that "to bring about true peace in accordance with divinely established order" was a "most noble task" (*Pacem in Terris*, V: *l.c.*, 301-302).

The fortieth anniversary of *Pacem in Terris* is an apt occasion to return to Pope John XXIII's prophetic teaching. Catholic communities will know how to celebrate this anniversary during the year with initiatives which, I hope, will have an ecumenical and interreligious character and be open to all those who have a heartfelt desire "to break through the barriers which divide them, to strengthen the bonds of mutual love, to learn to understand one another

90

and to pardon those who have done them wrong" (*l.c.*, 304).

I accompany this hope with a prayer to Almighty God, the source of all our good. May he who calls us from oppression and conflict to freedom and cooperation for the good of all help people everywhere to build a world of peace ever more solidly established on the four pillars indicated by Blessed Pope John XXIII in his historic Encyclical: *truth, justice, love, freedom.*

From the Vatican, 8 December 2002.

INDEX

VATICAN PRESS